Dentists

Quinn M. Arnold

seedlings

CREATIVE EDUCATION • CREATIVE PAPERBACKS

Published by Creative Education and Creative Paperbacks
P.O. Box 227, Mankato, Minnesota 56002
Creative Education and Creative Paperbacks
are imprints of The Creative Company
www.thecreativecompany.us

Design by Ellen Huber; production by Christine Vanderbeek
Art direction by Rita Marshall
Printed in the United States of America

Photographs by Alamy (CandyBox), iStockphoto (FatCamera), Shutterstock (Tatiana Chekryzhova, Chinnapong, el lobo, ESB Professional, Humannet, Dmitry Kalinovsky, kurhan, michaeljung, Monkey Business Images, Photosampler, Rocksweeper, Romas_Photo, Scott Rothstein, Silver Spiral Arts, Syda Productions, Kristijan Zontar)

Library of Congress Cataloging-in-Publication Data
Names: Arnold, Quinn M., author.
Title: Dentists / Quinn M. Arnold.
Series: Seedlings.
Includes index.
Summary: A kindergarten-level introduction to dentists, covering their job description, the places where they work, and how they help the community by keeping people's teeth healthy.
Identifiers: LCCN 2016059795
ISBN 978-1-60818-872-7 (hardcover)
ISBN 978-1-62832-487-7 (pbk)
ISBN 978-1-56660-920-3 (eBook)
Subjects: LCSH: 1. Dentistry—Juvenile literature. 2. Dentists—Juvenile literature. 3. Teeth—Care and hygiene—Juvenile literature.
Classification: LCC RK63.A76 2017 / DDC 617.6/0232—dc23
CCSS: RI.K.1, 2, 3, 4, 5, 6, 7;
RI.1.1, 2, 3, 4, 5, 6, 7; RF.K.1, 3; RF.1.1

First Edition HC 9 8 7 6 5 4 3 2 1
First Edition PBK 9 8 7 6 5 4 3 2 1

TABLE OF CONTENTS

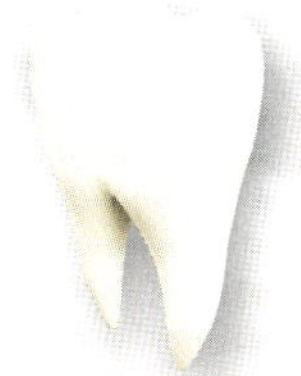

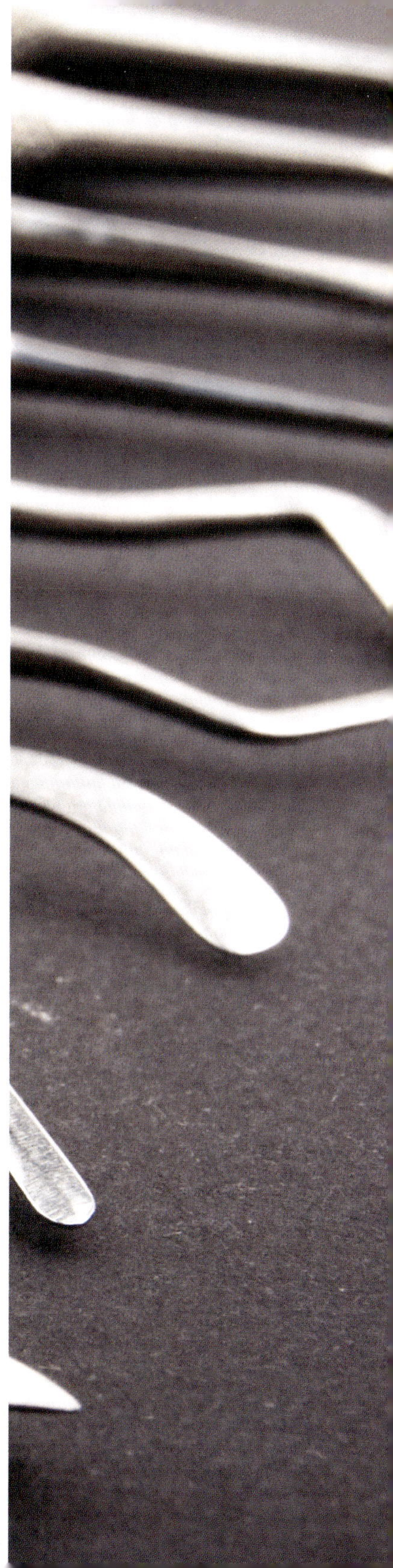

Hello, dentists!

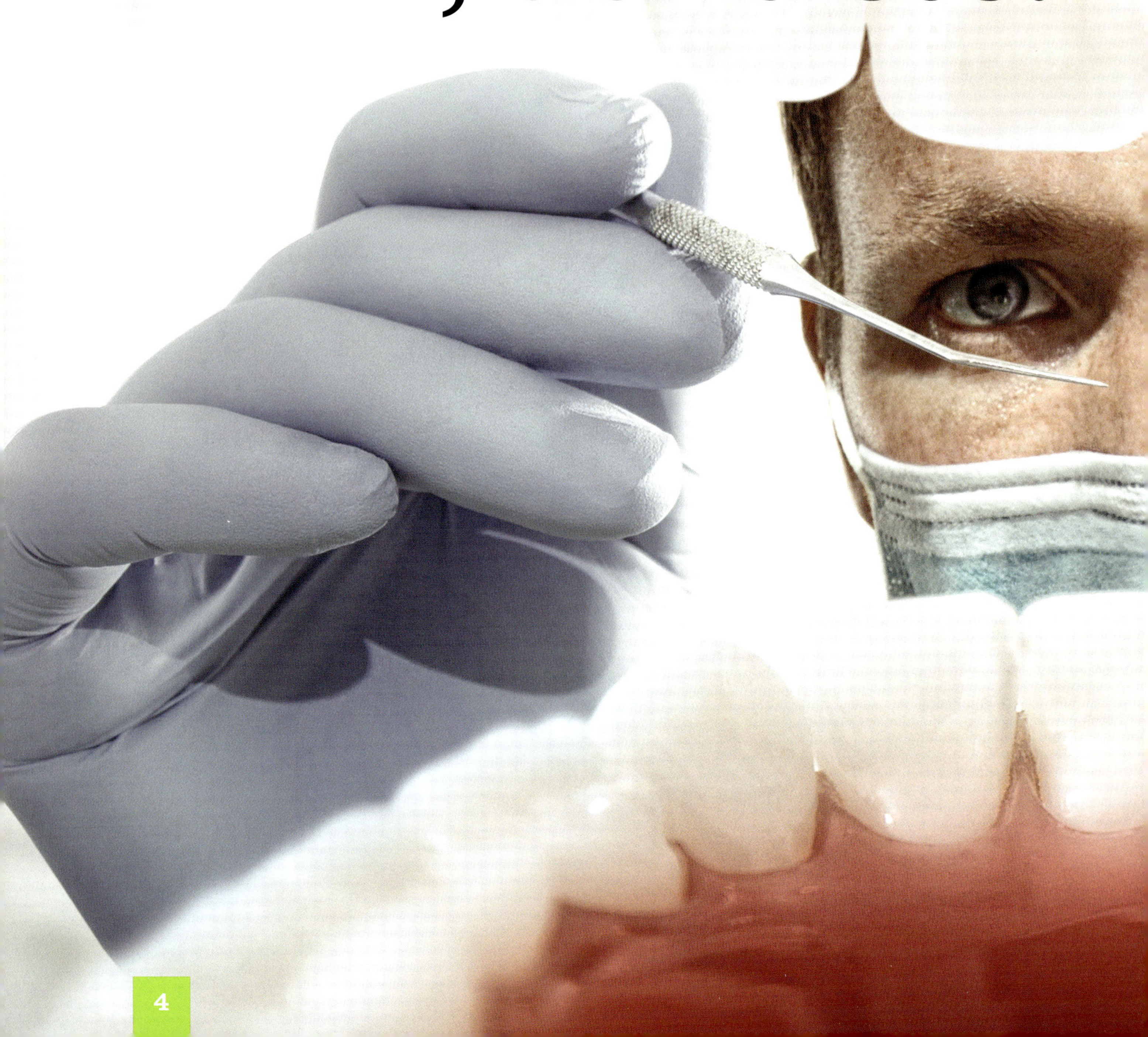

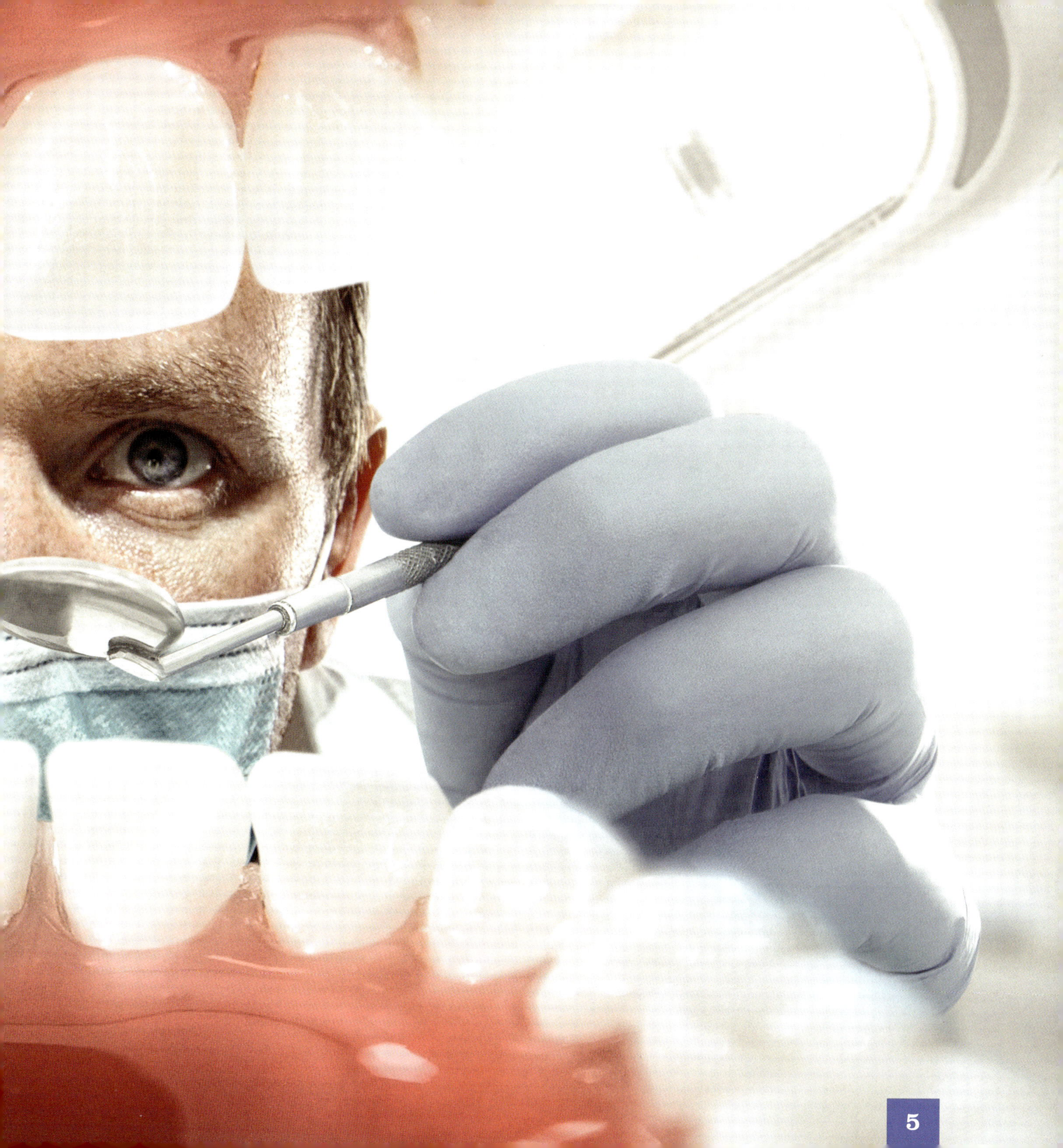

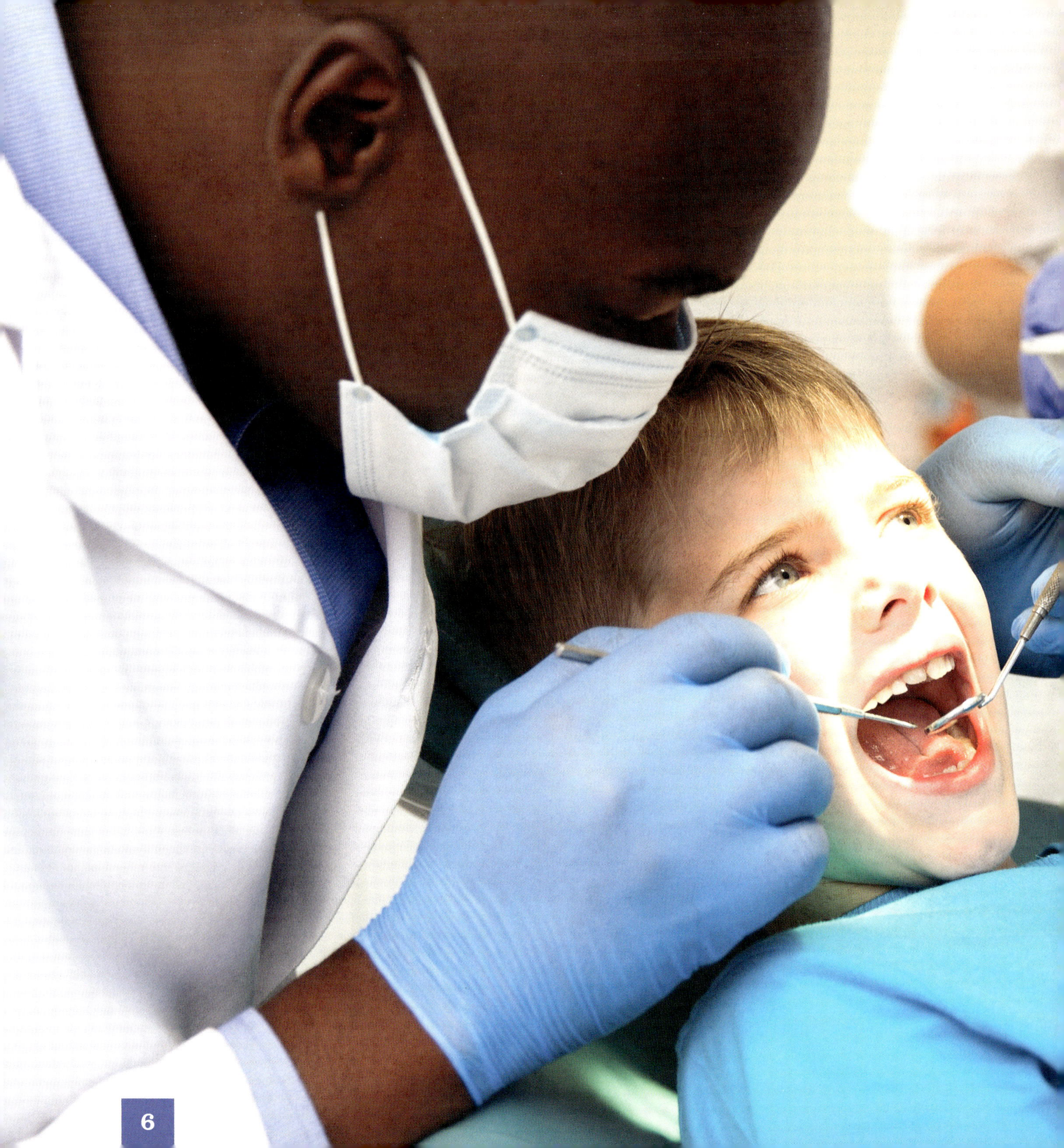

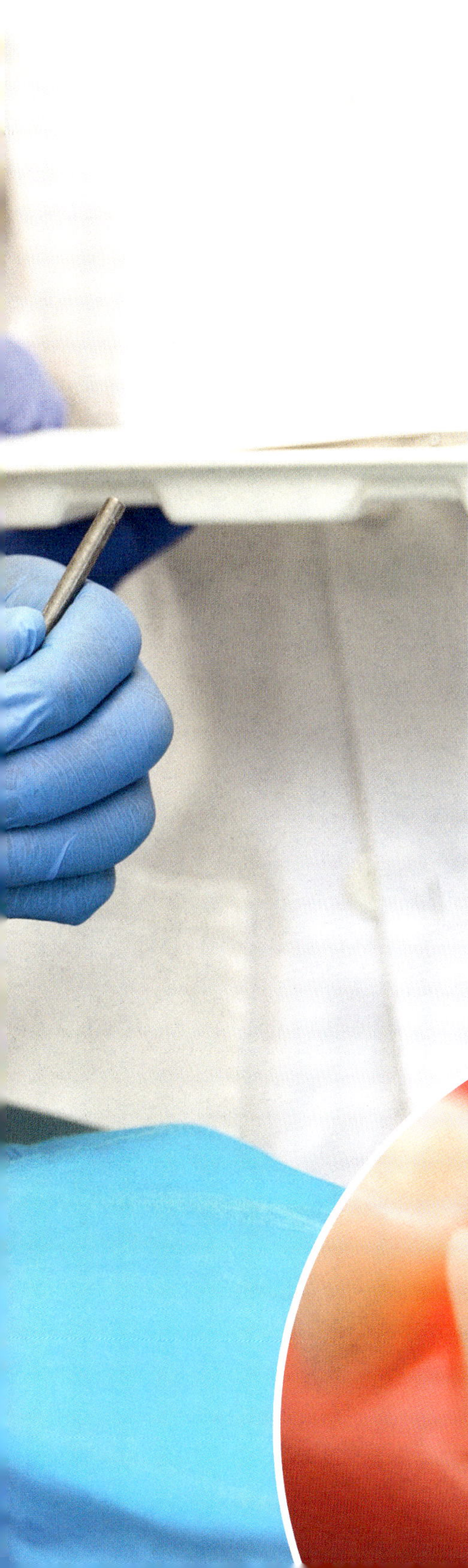

Dentists are doctors. They take care of people's mouths. They make sure the teeth and gums are healthy.

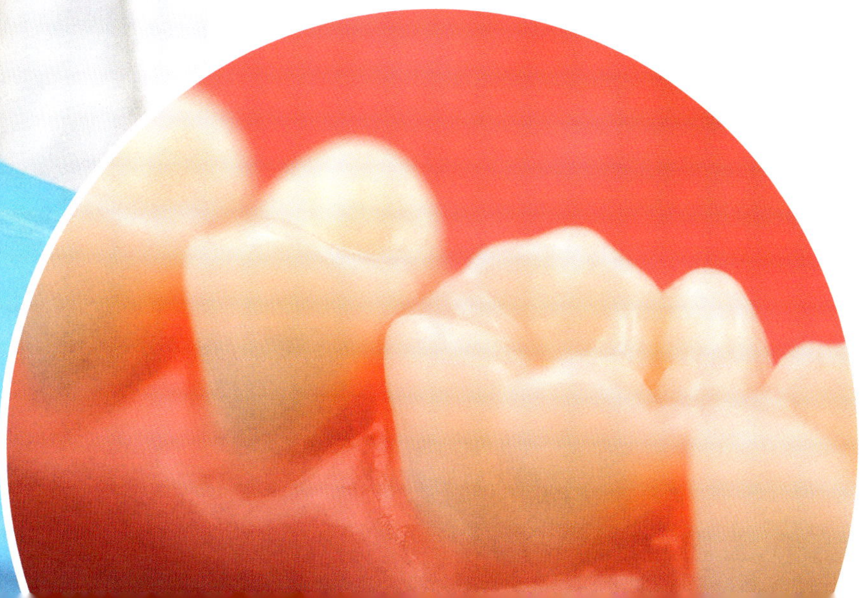

Most dentists work in an office. **Hygienists** help dentists. They clean teeth. They teach people how to brush and floss.

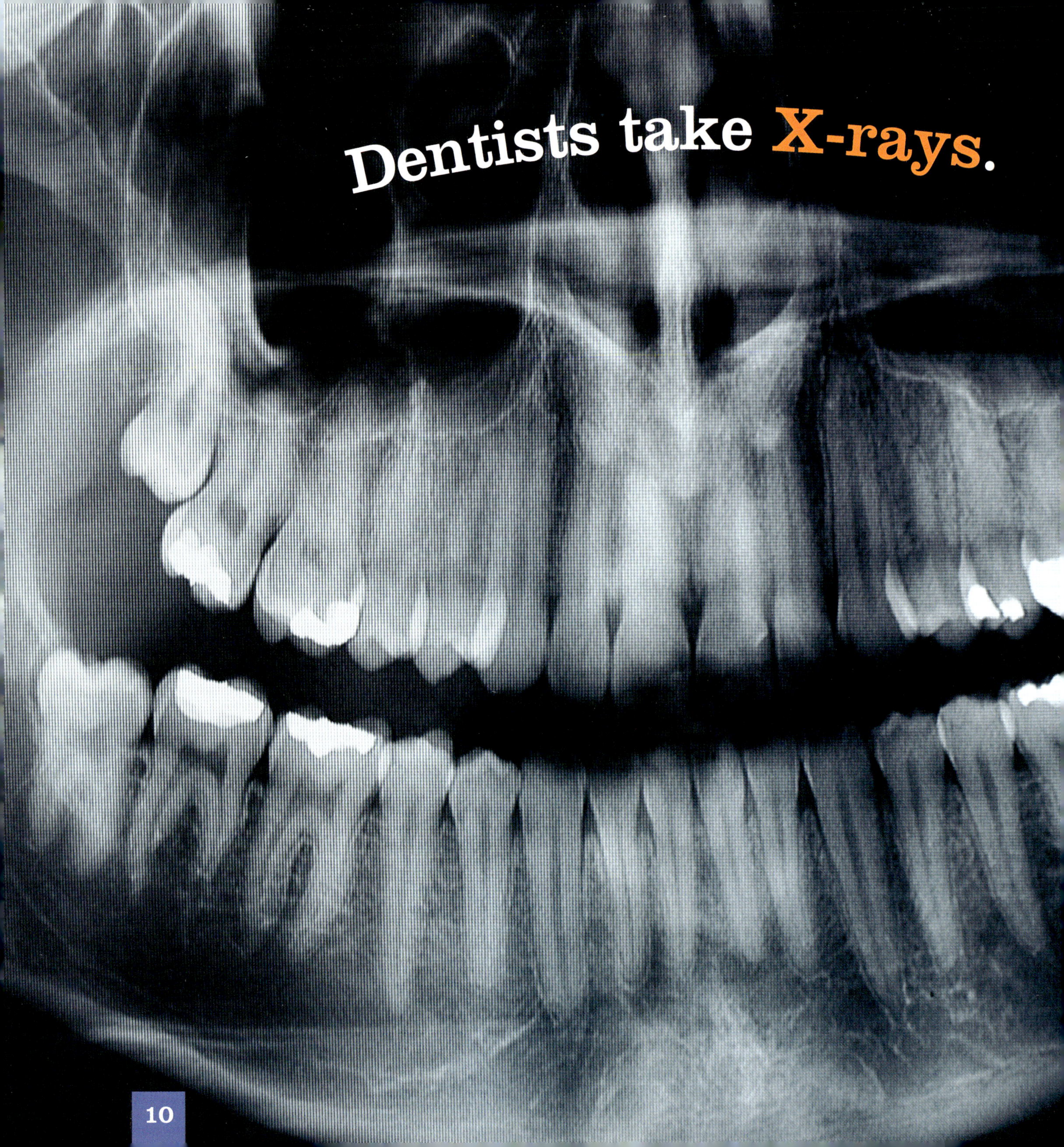

Dentists take X-rays.

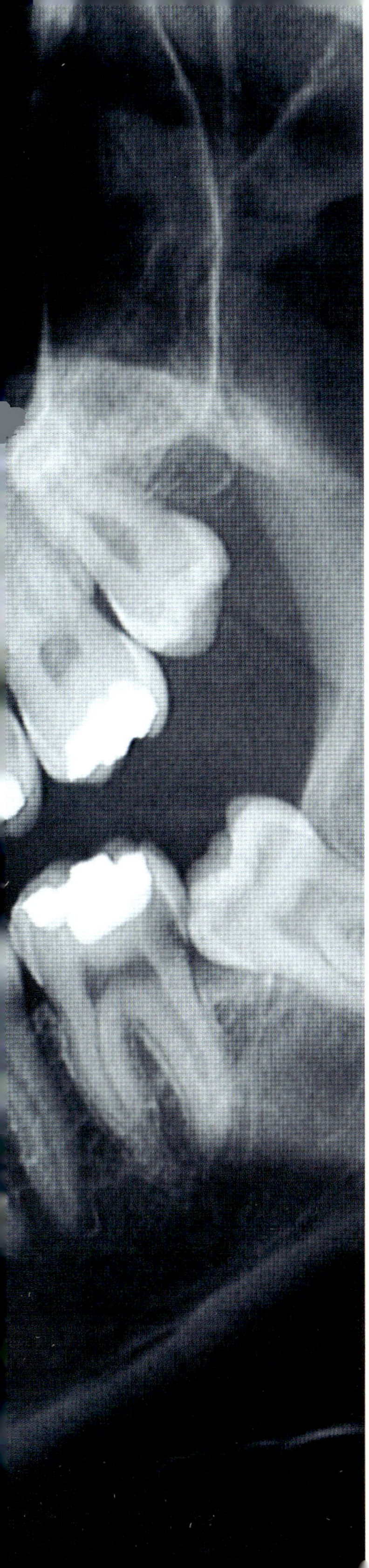

They fill in cavities. They fix teeth that are cracked. They pull loose teeth.

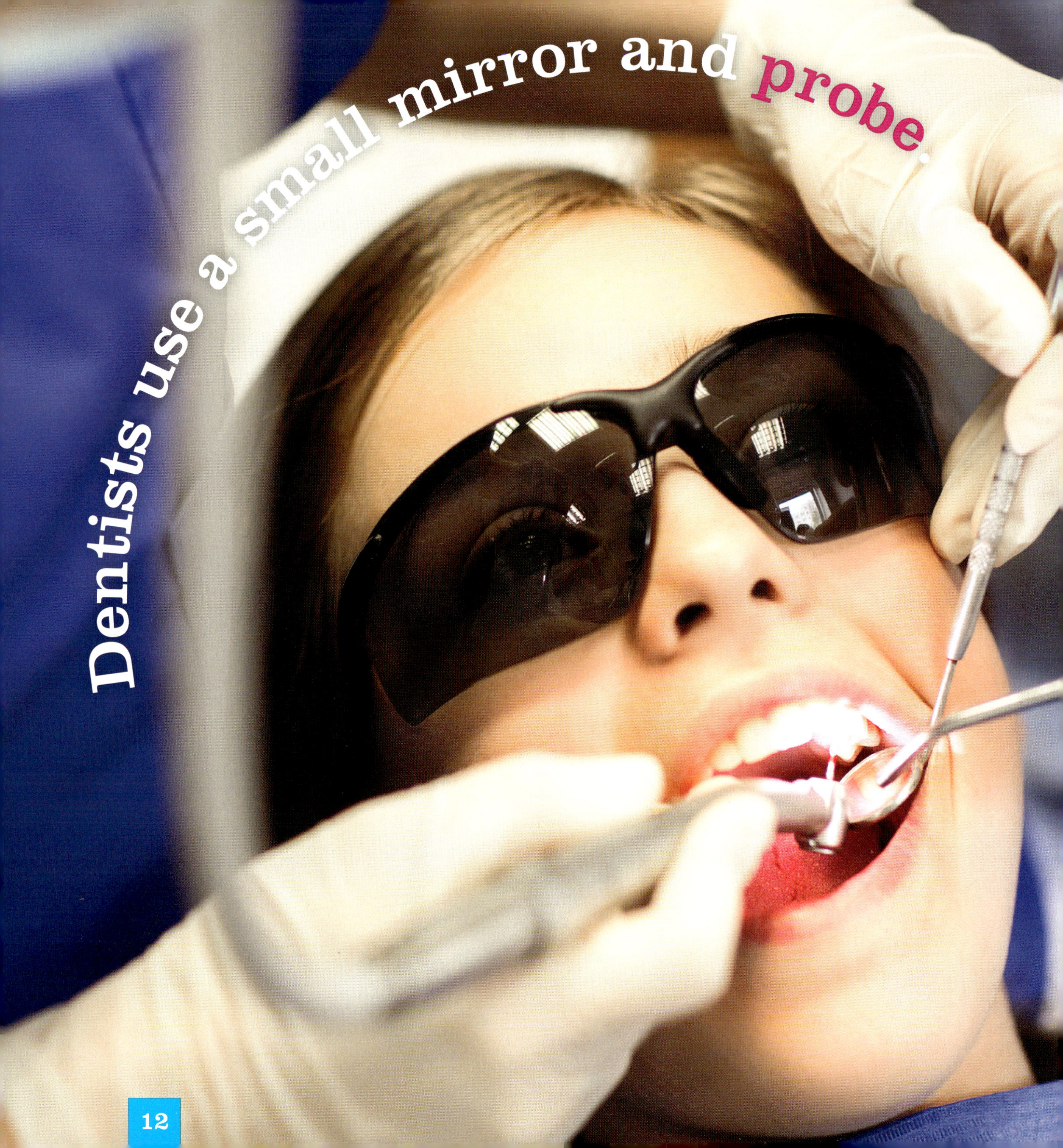

Dentists use a small mirror and **probe**.

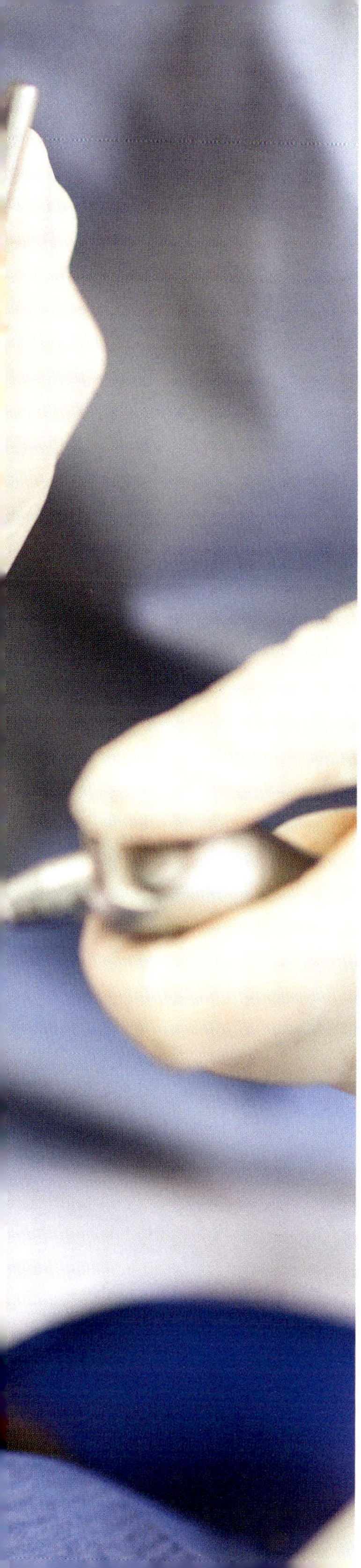

These help them see inside the mouth. Other tools help them fix teeth.

All dentists wear gloves and a mask as they work. Many wear a white coat, too.

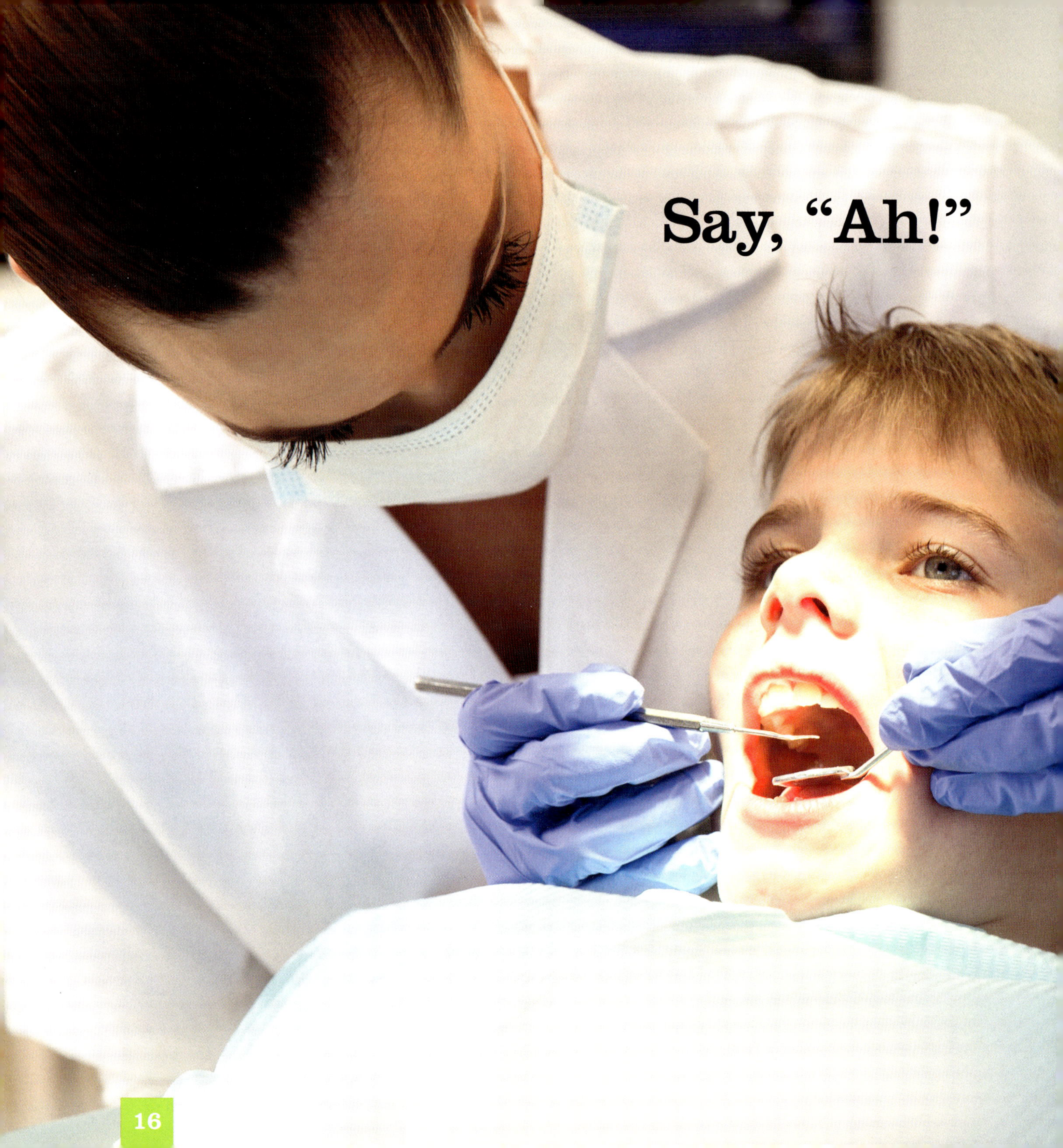

Say, "Ah!"

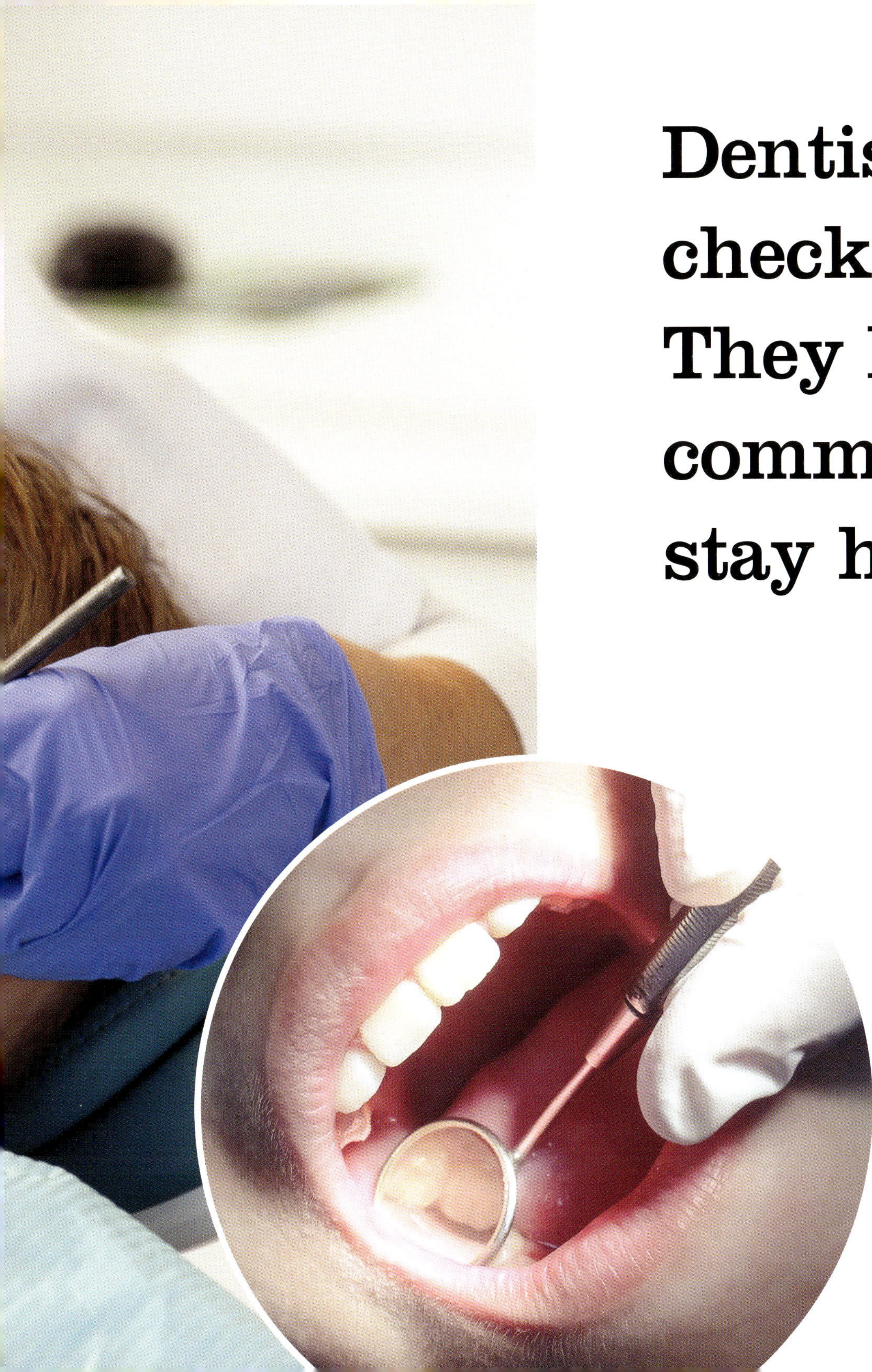

Dentists check teeth. They help communities stay healthy.

Goodbye, dentists!

Picture a Dentist

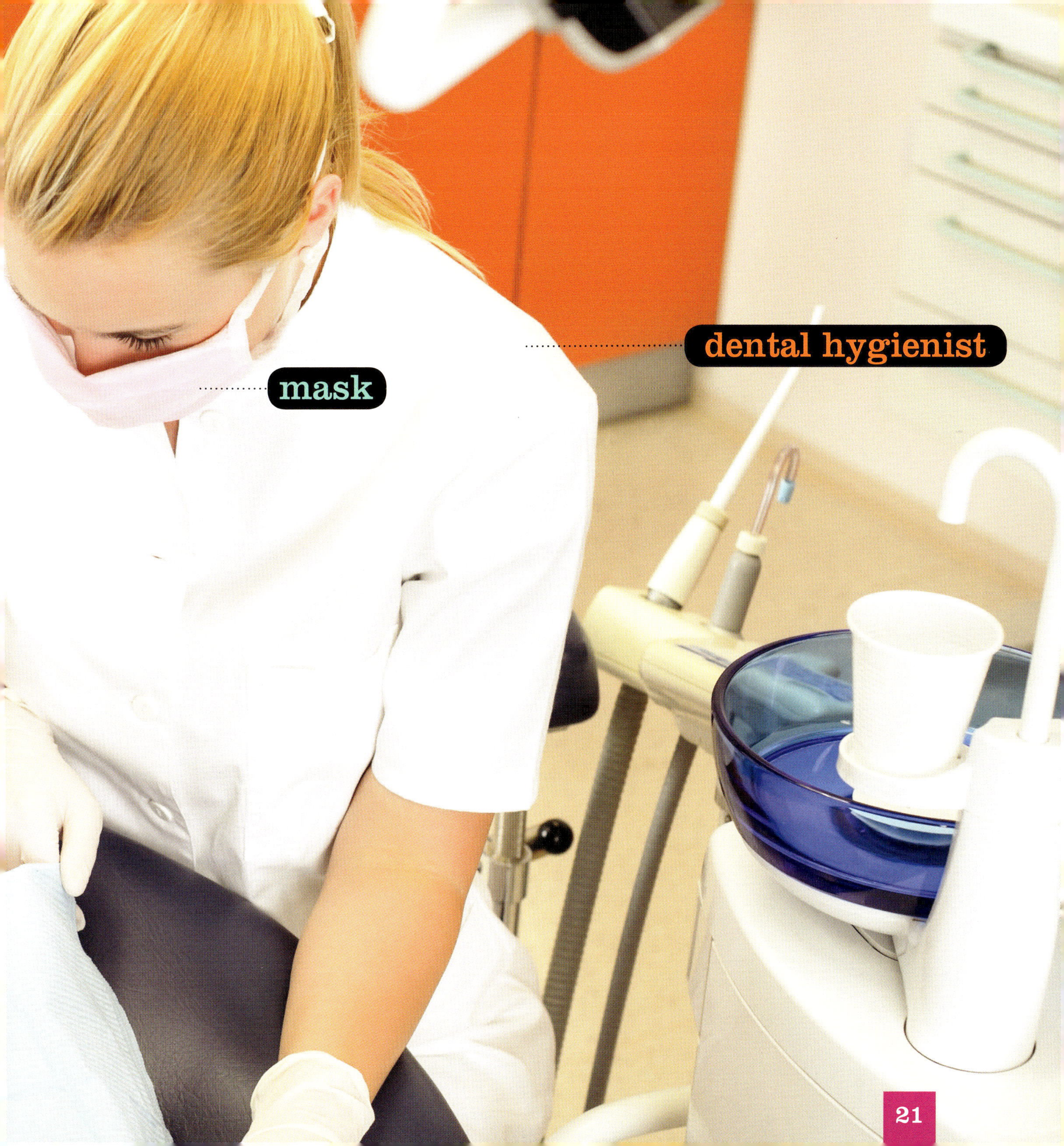
dental hygienist
mask

Words to Know

cavities: unhealthy parts of a tooth that are removed and filled in

hygienists: dental assistants who clean teeth

probe: a small medical tool used to look around an area

X-rays: pictures that show a person's bones, including teeth

Read More

Meister, Cari. *Dentists*. Minneapolis: Jump!, 2015.

Miller, Edward. *The Tooth Book: A Guide to Healthy Teeth and Gums*. New York: Holiday House, 2008.

Websites

Kids Health: Going to the Dentist
http://kidshealth.org/en/kids/go-dentist.html
Read more about what to expect at the dentist's office.

Mouth Healthy Kids
http://www.mouthhealthykids.org/en/
Play games, take quizzes, and learn how to keep your mouth healthy!

Note: Every effort has been made to ensure that the websites listed above are suitable for children, that they have educational value, and that they contain no inappropriate material. However, because of the nature of the Internet, it is impossible to guarantee that these sites will remain active indefinitely or that their contents will not be altered.

Index

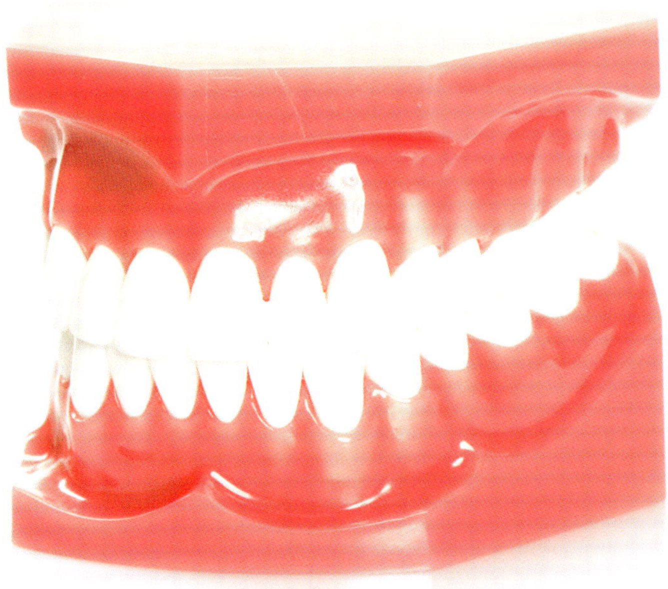